People inevitably ask me THE question,
"So, what do you do?"

"I free Gullivers."

FREE GULLIVER

SIX SWIFT LESSONS IN LIFE PLANNING

TRIPP FRIEDLER

FREE GULLIVER

Six Swift Lessons in Life Planning

TROST PUBLISHING

First Edition 2005

ISBN 1-933205-00-8

Manufactured in the United States of America

Library of Congress Control Number: 2004099411

Library of Congress Cataloging-in-Publication Data:

Friedler, Tripp.
Free Gulliver : six swift lessons in life planning /
Tripp Friedler. -- 1st ed.
p. cm.
ISBN 1-933205-00-8
1. Self-actualization (Psychology) 2. Life skills.
I. Title.

BF637.S4F745 2005   158
QBI04-200496

Design by Trumpet

To my dad, Frank Friedler, Jr., my mentor
and my best friend. I owe it all to you.

ACKNOWLEDGEMENTS

Where would I be without my terrific staff, Adam Fulk, Korrie Boerm, Deborah Bradbury, Katherine Moody, John Foster and Denise Guttenberg. Thank you for putting up with me on a daily basis. Also, to those who have come and gone, off to free their own Gullivers: Sara Schaefer, Jennifer Lewis and Stefanie Moss.

I must also thank two of the greatest editors a person could ask for, Sarah Doerries and Diana Pinckley.

I want to send a shout out to those of you who have given me ideas along the way: Emile Dumesnil, Robbie Vitrano, Henry O'Connor, Jim Swanson, Laura LeCorgne, Charles Marks, Andre Stern, Steve Cavanaugh, John McNamara, Dan Sullivan, Scott McLeod, Matt Leiberman, Randy Fertel, Josh Mayer and Sam Giberga.

To my agent, Evan Fogelman, who helped guide me through some perilous waters.

To Pam Friedler, who has a special place in heaven waiting for her.

Finally, to my wife Heidi and my three kids, Patti, Henry and Kate. Without you the journey would not be worth making.

INTRODUCTION

Do you ever feel trapped? Overwhelmed? Tied down? You're not alone.

Lemuel Gulliver, the protagonist of Jonathan Swift's *Gulliver's Travels*, survived a harrowing shipwreck only to be captured by the Lilliputians. How could this tiny race restrain the giant Gulliver? By tying him down with hundreds of little strings.

What's tying you down? An unfulfilling career? Financial instability? Not enough time for yourself or your family? Would you like to uncomplicate your life and start living your dream?

This is a story about freeing Gullivers, and it starts with the first Gulliver I freed: myself.

My journey toward freedom began when I graduated from law school in 1985 and went to work as an attorney for a large firm in New Orleans. It took me less than a year to realize that I needed to try another route. Working in a big law firm felt very much like working in a factory, and I needed something more entrepreneurial. So I joined my family's insurance business, where I was happy to work beside my father and grandfather. My grandfather had started a life insurance agency in 1929; by the time I joined in 1986, my father was in charge. He had converted the insurance company into a high-end financial and estate planning practice. My friends thought I was crazy for leaving behind the high salary of a lawyer for a job working purely on commission, but I enjoyed being part of a successful family tradition.

After a year or two, however, I realized that something was still missing from my life. I started to explore other venues, in search of that perfect niche where my passions met my profession. In 1989, Gautreau's Restaurant was on the market. My best friend was working at Gotham Bar and Grill, a renowned restaurant in New York City. We had always wanted to do something together, and this became our chance. Our version of Gautreau's opened in March, 1990, and we quickly turned it into one of the top restaurants in New Orleans. We served what we called Nouvelle French Cajun, and over the years we accumulated many honors, including having our pictures in *Time* magazine.

At around the same time, I happened to meet Chris

Blackwell, the founder of Island Records, and we struck up a friendship. Island had a great track record, having discovered such diverse artists as Bob Marley, U2, and Melissa Etheridge. While I loved music, I knew nothing about the music business. But, as Chris pointed out, I did know selling and marketing, so he convinced me to give it a try. After two hard years, I talked Island Records into signing a punk/zydeco band from Lafayette, Louisiana, called the BlueRunners. Our album was released on Island in 1991. This taste of the music business led me to become one of the founders of a record label, Monkey Hill, that enjoyed a few years of success with such New Orleans–based bands as Cowboy Mouth and The Continental Drifters.

Although these endeavors may seem glamorous and exciting, in my heart I was still an insurance sales-man. So I sold the restaurant in 1996, abandoned my music career, and returned to the family business. I felt lucky to both enjoy my profession and achieve success. I became involved in advising high-net-worth individuals about estate and financial planning, as well as helping corporations with incentive compensation and deferred compensation. My income was relatively high, and my life was busy. My grandfather retired at

92 years old, and my dad and I became partners. I was happy.

That happiness quickly faded when my father was diagnosed with Alzheimer's at age 63. The signs had been there for some time, but I had chosen to explain them away. When I could ignore them no longer, I was crushed. Not only was my father my mentor and partner, he was also my best friend. Anyone who has had a loved one suffer through Alzheimer's knows how tough it can be. I remember a walk Dad and I took where he told me he felt like an athlete who had plenty of good years left, but had suffered a career-ending injury. By the end of the walk, we were both crying.

DISCOVERING MY PASSION

After my father stopped working, I found myself alone in a business I had thought I loved. When I began to re-evaluate my life's work, I realized I loved the business because I was privileged to work in it with my dad, not because I had a passion for the insurance business itself. In fact, upon reflecting on all of my business choices, I realized that they were all connected by relationships. I had been in the restaurant business, the music business, and the insurance business because I wanted to work with the person that happened to be involved in that industry. Relationships were the passion that had helped drive my career.

My dad's illness forced me to focus on what was truly important to me—my family, my wife, myself—and I began to think about the things that tied me down. I realized that I had been chasing someone else's dream. **I needed to refocus and gain some clarity.**

I also realized that, in addition to working closely with those who were important in my life, my passion lay in helping people solve problems. Okay, so I discovered my passions. But I had no real vision of how they applied to my career, until I began to think hard about how to change my business. The financial services industry provides many valuable products, but I was tired of a product-driven business model. Over time, and following a good bit of thought, I developed a vision—to create a business that helps people align their financial dreams with their life dreams. Through this process, I realized that I could slow down, enjoy life, spend more time with my family, and still accomplish my business and financial goals.

Realizing it and doing it were two different things. It is always easier to see what needs to be done than it is to actually do it. I knew my idea for a new business would work, but I also knew that it would take time and money to accomplish my goals. In *Good to Great*, Jim Collins talks about "the Stockdale paradox." This is having the unshakable belief that one will succeed regardless of the obstacles *and* at the same time having the discipline to confront the reality of one's current situation. Collins named the paradox after Admiral James Stockdale, the highest-ranking United States military officer in the Hanoi Hilton prisoner of war camp in Vietnam. Admiral Stockdale survived while being tortured repeatedly over his eight-year imprisonment. It is truly a remarkable story. Stockdale tells Collins that of all the prisoners in the camp, the optimists were the ones who did not survive. Stockdale explains,

"…Oh, they were the ones who said, 'We're going to be out by Christmas.' And then Christmas would come, and Christmas would go. Then they'd say, 'We're going to be out by Easter.' And Easter would come, and Easter would go. And then Thanksgiving, and then it would be Christmas again. And they died of a broken heart…"

The lesson Stockdale gathered from this experience was that one must never confuse the belief that you will ultimately prevail, which must exist, with the resolve to confront the reality of your current situation.

MAKING THE LEAP

So in 2000, I was stuck in the middle of my own Stockdale paradox. I knew I needed to follow my dream, but I also knew this would mean a severe short term cut in pay. I needed to make a big change and I was scared.

Change is always scary. Anytime your status quo is altered, fear and anxiety are often lurking behind. I remember being in a room full of entrepreneurs once, when the speaker asked what "normal" meant to us. The whole room responded with answers such as "dull" and "boring." The fact is that normal simply means, "that to which we feel accustomed." The way you are currently living is what is normal for you. It is normal for the President to wake up every day in the White House. It is normal for Tom Cruise to see himself on movie screens around the world. Each of us has our own "normal." In this book, I am asking you to experience a "new normal." I completely understand that this is difficult to do. It is impossible to go from a familiar normal to a new normal without fear and anxiety.

In his 1987 book, *The Structure of Individual Psychotherapy*, Bernard Beitman refers to the area between normals as "the great abyss." This is the perfect metaphor. The image of an intimidating bottomless pit helps us understand why we are threatened by change. Not one of us wants to fall into the great abyss, yet all of us must gather up the courage to make the leap across it if we are to grow.

So, I was forced to make my own leap. I had done it before—when I gave up the practice of law to go into the insurance business, when I bought the restaurant, when I started the label—and yet here I was, at age 39, doing it again.

FREEING GULLIVERS

Around this time, my client Randy sold his family business for a fair amount of money. At the time, he was employing a part-time bookkeeper but clearly needed more help. My background in finance combined with my law degree, I thought, would be perfect credentials for me to help Randy with his business. He agreed and became my first client in my new venture.

It was 1999 and the dot-com business was in full swing. My idea was to be a one-stop shop for wealthy families, where I could deal with insurance, investments, tax issues, lawyers, and other things that would help them simplify their lives. I would use the Internet as a resource to allow them access to up-to-the-minute information and records. I had tried coming up with names for my venture on my own, to no avail.

So I met my friend Josh for lunch. Josh, one of the most imaginative people I know, is creative head of his family's advertising agency, which he has helped to grow into the largest in the region. I explained to him what my new concept was, and after a few lunches, Josh threw out the name "Free Gulliver." After all, he reasoned, my clients were like Gulliver, tied down by all their advisors, and I could free them. I loved it. My company had a name.

These were exciting times, and my business began to take off. By 2000, I had four or five clients and began to realize I had stumbled into a great niche. I also started to understand that my clients were tied down by strings of a somewhat different nature than I had initially thought. Certainly they appreciated the assistance with their finances and with coordinating the various professionals involved. However, where they really seemed to need help was in gaining clarity about why they did what they did. They were all so busy running in the great race we call life, they had lost their way. They needed clarity, just as I had a few months earlier. This is best summarized by a brief encounter I had with a friend who had recently been "downsized." For those of you who have first-hand experience, you know how crushing this can be. My friend was no exception; all her plans were "destroyed." She was distraught. So I asked her one question, "Where is your finish line?"

This is an important question, and one most of my clients had never contemplated. Why do we all feel like we need to achieve our goals as quickly as possible? We forget that half the fun is the journey itself. My friend still had her goals, which were all still achievable. It was just going to take a little longer for her to get there, at least financially. But as long as she was enjoying the trip, what's a few more years? And it's a trip that she might enjoy even more without the pressures of her former job. I convinced her to move back her financial "finish line" a few years, and she was back on course.

After helping a few clients work toward their own clarity, I decided that one more degree would give me the foundation I needed for this new part of my career. I went back to school and now am almost finished earning my master's in counseling. Today, *FreeGulliver* is a company of seven people. Among us, we have graduate degrees in business, finance, law, social work, and (coming soon) counseling and international development. We've developed a unique process that helps our clients, both individual and corporate, gain clarity. Much of this process is outlined in this book.

There. That leap across the great abyss wasn't nearly as bad as I had imagined it would be. It did take me a couple of years (and some debt) to get my income back to where I needed it. But one unforgettable season, I looked behind me and realized that I had successfully made the transition from the familiar to the "new normal."

In the fall of 2002, I coached my ten-year-old son's soccer team. I had always been too busy to coach my children's teams; I was interested, but I never thought I'd have the time. I decided that this was the year to change, to free myself from my time constraints and participate in something that was important to me. I'm sure my son enjoyed the experience, but his delight paled in comparison to mine. We had a blast and even won the championship.

That's when I knew for sure I had freed my first Gulliver. **I had freed myself.**

This book will explore the tools I used to free myself, tools I use now to free my clients. The key is **clarity**, an amazingly intense force that is surprisingly easy to attain—as long as you know where to look.

Attaining clarity begins with identifying your **vision**—of yourself and your future. In order to plan your journey and stick to the right course, you must have an accurate image of who you are and where you want to go.

The next step is to assess where you are right now. It is impossible to get anywhere without knowing your current location—in terms of life goals and financial goals. Yet many people will make major life decisions without having a clear picture of where they are.

Next, we will discuss your **passions**. What are the

things that are most important to you? What do you love to do? What is your real drive? I give my clients a series of questions that produce what I refer to as their "passion statement," a declaration of their genuine, innate passions. My passion statement is simple: "I want to free Gullivers."

Finally, I ask you to visualize what you want to leave behind after your life's journey is finished. That is your **legacy**. How do you want to be remembered? Who do you want to provide for? Do you want to live a legacy or leave one? How can you start living your legacy today—with your family, your finances, your community? Envisioning the end of your journey will inspire your life and allow you to make clear decisions, now and in the future.

Once you have established your vision (destination), location (starting point), and passion (fuel) you're ready to apply them to your life strategies—and to the basic financial planning and estate planning strategies that will help you attain your vision. Specifically, we will discuss **risk** and how it relates to your decisions, and we will re-evaluate the idea of **retirement**. Along the way, we will take a look at a number of Gullivers who have already been freed. You'll see how they worked themselves loose from the ties that bound them and succeeded in pursuing their passions, thus prospering.

So, get ready to be untied—get ready to free your Gulliver!

VISION

John F. Kennedy did not live to see the fulfillment of the vision that he set in motion when he proclaimed on May 25, 1961, "I believe that this nation should commit itself to achieving the goal, before this decade is out, of landing a man on the moon and returning him safely to Earth." This daunting task required enormous funds and mandated great technological advances, but Congress did not hesitate to pursue it. Kennedy's vision touched on America's enduring passions: leadership and the pioneering spirit. In the same era, civil rights pioneer Martin Luther King, Jr. expressed his vision to the nation in his "I Have a Dream" speech. What would our world be like today if Kennedy and King had never conceived and articulated their visions?

In our process, vision is the idea you have of what you want your life to look like, of your long-term goals. Think of your vision as a guiding light on your path to success. The definition of success here is completely relative. Success for me may mean raising a happy, healthy family, but your success may have more to do with running a profitable restaurant. Your vision should be based on who you are, on your passions and potential. It should be a source of inspiration and guidance. Don't be afraid to extend yourself when composing your vision statement; **you'll never be greater than the vision that guides you.**

Identifying your vision allows you to consider who you are, to reevaluate your worldview. The process requires genuine introspection and an evaluation of what is important to you. As you will learn in the following lessons, identifying your vision, passion, and location will create clarity in your life. This clarity will open all kinds of doors and help you close the ones that lead you astray.

Answering the following questions might be helpful in creating your occupational vision:

Imagine your work life in 10 years. Ideally, what does it look like?

What do you do?

_____

_____

_____

List your work hours.

How successful are you on a scale from 1 to 10?
(10 being very successful)

Name your position/title.

My vision started to become clear when I realized my disillusionment with the financial services industry. I began to search for a better way to provide value for my clients. I felt that the industry was too focused on products, ignoring the opportunities to provide valuable solutions that may or may not involve product sales. My vision, at least in the professional realm, is nothing short of transforming an industry—one client at a time. People can achieve any goal they realistically and clearly set. I'm sure of it. That's why my vision is to help everyone achieve the type of clarity that I have been able to create.

L Y N E T T E

Lynette lacked a vision when she came to see me. Lynette was CEO of a very successful company that she had helped to build from the ground up. She had recently received a large bonus from her employer and needed help investing it. The amount was of such magnitude that Lynette figured she could quit working in another five years. Thus she was putting a lot of pressure on herself to invest wisely. Lynette loved her job but felt the time was coming for her to leave it. She had done all she could for the company, and her successor was ready to be promoted. Lynette's husband, Roger, a teacher, was enthusiastic about her retire-in-five-years plan because he wanted to travel more.

After a few meetings, I began to press Lynette about her vision of her future. What were her long-term goals? This brought out some interesting discussions. It seemed that while Lynette wanted to travel, she also longed to be active in business. She had a vision of being a CEO in a larger business and bringing her style of management onto a bigger playing field. She wanted to be able to effect change in a more meaningful way. We are now working on an investment plan that leaves

Lynette enough room to take a year off, travel with Roger, reinvigorate, and move on to the next challenge.

CHOOSING THE ROAD

This lack of vision is not isolated strictly to individuals. One of my corporate clients is rebranding itself, with the help of a great agency, as part of a new advertising campaign. The agency brought me in to help bring clarity to the vision of the company. It is impossible to project something you are not. Before any company can brand itself to the outside world, it needs to brand itself internally. It needs a vision.

Remember *Alice in Wonderland*? At one point, Alice comes to a crossroads. She is confused because she does not know which road to take. She meets the Cheshire Cat there and asks him what to do. He inquires where she wants to go; she replies that she does not know. "Well then," he says, "any road will take you there." No truer words have ever been spoken. If you do not know your vision, if you're unclear about where you want to go, all too often you will take the Cheshire Cat's advice and believe that any choice is a good one.

Nothing could be further from the truth. In order to make good choices, it is critical to know where you want to go. You must have a vision.

My client and I spent time with the corporate senior management team, reconnecting everyone to a common vision. The vision did not have to be sold to the team, because it came from them. With this vision in clear focus, the choice of roads has become apparent.

MICHAEL

Finally, there is the story of Michael. Michael was a 45-year-old lawyer who was very good at what he did. In fact, national surveys constantly acclaimed him as one of the best lawyers in his field anywhere. He was making more money than he ever thought possible. To the rest of the world, he had the perfect life. He was married to a great woman, had two beautiful kids, and was well respected in his profession. The only problem was that Michael was not happy. He had a different vision. He wanted to be an entrepreneur. He wanted to start his own business. He wanted more time with his kids. There is a great quote from M. Scott Peck that says, "Success eliminates as many options as does failure." Michael was living proof of this. We sat down and I began to ask him questions. He did the exercises in this book. We decided that his vision was all about business, and only tangentially related to law. He formulated a new set of goals and we began to create the strategies that will accomplish them. Michael is currently on a road illuminated by his vision and is happier for it.

Michael was able to clearly answer the following questions. Can you?

Picture your personal life in 10 years. Ideally, what does it look like?

Are you in a relationship?

Do you have children? How old are they?

Where are you living?

Do you take vacations? If so, where?

In my practice the number of people I see, like Michael, who stay with something just because "they are good at it," amazes me. Just because you are good at something does not mean you should be doing it. I constantly focus on getting my clients to clarify their vision of success as defined by their passions, not their competencies. These two often go hand in hand, but it is important to be aware of the differences.

I realize that not everyone will be able to abandon their career just because it does not fit in their vision. That's okay. There may be many reasons to stay in a job that you are good at, but do not love, like prestige or a high salary. Only you can decide if these reasons justify your staying. All I am saying is that you do have choices and you owe it to yourself to consider them carefully.

If your vision is inspiring enough, it can generate the energy needed for its own fulfillment. If you see how your work supports and contributes to the "big picture" (your vision), your work will seem more meaningful and can be more directed. Your vision may provide clarity in times of distress. **You have to**

know *why* before you can decide *what*.

Using this lesson as a guide, formulate your own occupational and personal vision.

List your complete 10-year vision for yourself below.

In 10 years I will be...

_____

_____

_____

_____

_____

2
LESSON

LOCATION

Being entirely honest with oneself is a good exercise.
—Sigmund Freud

Before beginning any journey, you need to know your point of departure. I was recently at a corporate client retreat and I dared anyone in the room to get a flight to New Orleans without telling the airline their city of departure. It cannot be done. No matter what your destination, the first key to getting there is knowing where you already are. Remember "the Stockdale paradox" from the introduction, which is based on knowing all of the facts of your current reality. In other words, know your location. Which decisions have brought you success and happiness? Which ones have led to disappointment and frustration?

CAROLINE

Caroline, an attractive and energetic woman in her late fifties whose husband had recently died, needed someone to help her plan her affairs. Her husband had been an extremely successful businessman and had left her ample means to live without any financial concerns. Caroline's passion was gardening, and she and her husband had found a way to translate that passion into a profession: an herb business. Caroline enjoyed running the small company, which allowed her all the free time she needed. We worked on a passion statement and discovered that she wished she had more time to spend with her grandchildren and more time to travel.

When Caroline told me her plans to go into the restaurant business, I was stunned. I asked Caroline why she was interested in trying out a new business. I knew from my own experience how difficult it is to run a restaurant—it's definitely not the kind of work you want to plunge into late in life, especially if you don't need the money and want more free time.

We began to review how Caroline had arrived at her current location. She had worked all her life, been married, divorced, and remarried. It was only when her second husband died that she acquired great wealth—money she had inherited, not earned. Caroline realized that she felt guilty about her inheritance; she had always worked hard for her successes, and this was one she felt she didn't deserve. Her desire to start her own business began to make sense. The restaurant was her attempt to justify her wealth.

PAST TENSE?

Knowing where you are is important, but you must have genuine clarity about how you got there in order to make sound decisions. Where you've been can affect your choices just as strongly as where you are. Remember, objects in your rearview mirror may be closer than they appear. Your past may play a bigger role in your present than you realize. Caroline came to realize that she didn't need superfluous projects to justify her financial situation; she could continue to run her herb business and enjoy extra time with her grandchildren, which, as we'll discuss later, leaves a family legacy at least as valuable as a vast estate. How big a role is your past playing? The following exercise might help you figure this out.

List some spending/saving habits of your parents.

Mother

_____

_____

_____

Father

_____

_____

_____

I G N O R A N C E = F E A R

Many of my clients are out of touch with where they are financially. These are smart people with one thing in common: they do not want to know their current financial situation. They fear that such knowledge will limit their options. You know what I'm talking about: the idea that anything is possible as long as you don't let the facts get in the way. But there's only one fact that really matters. When it comes to finances, you are where you are whether you know it or not. You may have student loans, credit-card debt, or a car worth less than the amount you owe on it. These can all be painful, difficult situations, but ignoring them will not make them go away. Which would you prefer: to be in control of your debt, or to have your debt control you?

Ignorance of your current financial situation will truly limit your options. Clarity creates opportunity, and with opportunity comes options. The key to success is to make informed, educated decisions. Imagine the power of knowing exactly what you're doing and why; imagine knowing exactly where you stand and using that knowledge as a guide. Choices made out of ignorance come with a price: fear. How many times have you put a luxury—a new TV or vacation, for example—on a credit card? You knew you didn't have the money to pay for these items, but, by ignoring the facts, you were able to do as you pleased. I'm not suggesting that you never treat yourself to a luxury. In fact, I encourage just the opposite. But if you take an inventory of your present situation, you'll know how to adjust in other areas so you can make that purchase without worry. It may well be that you can indulge in first-class flights and five-star hotels. But how can you know for sure without a real understanding of your financial situation? If you have clarity, you will be able to make educated choices and thus pursue your dreams with confidence.

CHARLES

Charles was facing a tough decision. He could not afford to send his three children to private schools through twelfth grade and fund their college careers. He found himself in the same quandary as many middle-class families. He was making too much to qualify for financial aid, but not enough to afford private school tuition and still be able to save for college. He also wasn't sure if he could count on merit-based scholarships. He did not want to risk his kids not qualifying for aid based on his income and then not getting any academic scholarships as well. While he struggled to find a solution, Charles continued to sink further and further into debt trying to finance the high cost of tuition. He came to me with his dilemma, already prepared with some well-thought-out ideas.

Charles took inventory of his current financial situation, and we did some projecting based on increasing tuition costs. Unfortunately, we could find no way for Charles to afford private school and college tuition for all three kids. Charles researched the public schools in his area, chose the ones he believed would provide the best education to his children, and got them enrolled. He started to save and invest the money he would have spent on private schools, with a strategy that planned for his children's future college-tuition needs. By choosing knowledge over ignorance, Charles was able to replace inaction with action, debt with savings, and fear of the future with confidence.

NORMAN

As a contrast I offer the story of Norman. He went to one of the best private schools in his city and excelled far beyond his classmates. In his senior year, he was accepted to both Princeton and Yale. Norman's classmates celebrated his success; they all had witnessed his cool genius in class and his ability to lead in sports, extracurricular activities and student government. When the list of graduates' chosen colleges was published, everyone was surprised to see that Norman was enrolled in an enormous state school known more for its sports and partying than for its academics. Norman was forced to surrender his dream of the Ivy League because his parents had not planned ahead: they had overextended themselves paying private-school tuition and did not have any money in reserve to pay the Ivy League schools' high tuition. The apparent advantages afforded by private secondary school had robbed him of his ultimate goal.

DOLLARS AND SENSE

As these two cases clearly demonstrate, understanding your financial situation is fundamental to making wise spending decisions. By ignoring the facts, you create not opportunities but disappointments. Ignorance leads at best to false hope, at worst to insecurity. Knowledge allows for real opportunities and confidence. It's never too late to figure out where you are and start drawing a map leading to where you want to go. These questions can help.

List some of the best money decisions you have made.

_____

_____

_____

_____

List some of the worst money decisions you have made.

_____

_____

_____

_____

It's time for you to get clear about where you are financially. Let's start with your assets, those items you own that have value on the open market. Don't worry if your list of assets is short. Do not include routine household items such as clothes, furniture, appliances, or anything else of that nature. Who are you trying to kid? Unless you plan on actually selling all your personal possessions and living in a monastery, why bother even including them? Remember, the job at hand is to get an accurate picture of your current situation. It may be difficult, but your goal is to understand reality, not perpetuate fantasy. This worksheet should help you get there.

ASSETS	LIABILITIES
Marketable Securities _____	Mortgage _____
Home _____	Credit Cards _____
Other Real Estate _____	Car Note _____
Cash _____	Student Loans _____
Other _____	Other _____
Total Assets _____	Total Liabilities _____

The assets you should pay the closest attention to are your *liquid assets*—cash or items that can easily and quickly be exchanged for cash, such as stocks and bonds. Illiquid assets are items such as real estate, business interests and partnerships. Although their value is convertible to cash, they may require a longer time for conversion or carry a penalty for conversion prior to their maturity date. For instance, a house may be appraised at $300,000, but it might take six months or more to sell it for that amount.

Now let's examine your *net worth.* Net worth is simply the value of your assets, both liquid and illiquid, minus the value of your debts. Remember this: Do not confuse net worth with self worth. In our materialistic society, it's natural for people to think themselves worthless based on a deficient financial situation. Do not let this stop you from getting an accurate picture of your current net worth. Try not to compare yourself to others. Be thankful for who you are and what you do have, but resist the urge to remain ignorant of your true net worth.

Total Net Worth

_____

(Total Assets minus Total Liabilities)

Once you know how much money you have to spend, you should create a budget that helps you spend it responsibly. That makes sense, doesn't it? So why don't we all make budgets? Because a budget shows us, in no uncertain terms, what we can and cannot afford. When your friends are bragging about their new car or luxurious vacation, you may be tempted to hide your budget at the bottom of the trash can. Why shouldn't you have whatever you want? Life is short. Besides, as the salesperson will tell you, it's not what the car or vacation costs that matters—it's what they cost per month. This fallacy is the salesperson's best friend: they'll just keep breaking down the cost until it sounds affordable. Knowledge of your passion and clarity of vision are powerful weapons against this kind of manipulation. As long as these two important principles remain the cornerstone of your plan, you won't stray too far off course. After all, as the saying goes, "It's not having what you want, it's wanting what you have." And if you really want that expensive new car, you can have it, but it might mean fewer nights out until the bill is paid. It's your choice.

As you begin to implement your financial plan, it's smart to reassess your location from time to time. Now that you've established your current location you may be tempted to delegate your plan to an accountant or financial planner. Do not fall into this trap. You need to continually update where you are, where you want to go, and what you have (and need) to get there. I meet with clients quarterly to review their plans; at a minimum, you should review your assets annually to see if your situation has changed. If you don't, you run the risk of wasting valuable time. Remember, time is money—and, of course, money is money. Your objective should be to have enough of each to accomplish your goals.

Take some time to carefully answer the questions

below. This will help you pinpoint your location on the map of your life.

Do you have a will?

_____

Do you have an estate plan?

_____

Have you established trusts for your children?

_____

Currently I have an annual earned income of approximately $

_____

Currently I have an unearned income of approximately $

_____

Currently I have assets of approximately $

_____

To be financially comfortable, I need annual income of $

_____

and assets of $

_____

Based on this information, how do you think you are doing?

☐ **Very Poorly**   ☐ **Poorly**   ☐ **OK**

☐ **Well**   ☐ **Very Well**

LESSON

3

PASSION

*The happiness of a man in this life does not consist
in the absence but in the mastery of his passions.*
—Lord Alfred Tennyson

After understanding your vision and location, the next step in freeing your Gulliver is discovering what drives you—your passion. It is important to know why you do what you do. This understanding is the foundation of your passion statement, an essential element toward the goal of clarity. Passion involves intensity of feeling, a strong emotion with a compelling effect. James Hillman, author of *The Soul's Code: In Search of Character and Calling*, believes that passion is "not an action, an intention; rather it is a reaction, a being moved, a passio." In other words, passion is not something you can control—it controls you. It is the energy that will propel you in your quest toward your vision. It is your fuel.

Early in my career, a woman I met at a cocktail party asked me that all-important question: **"What do you do?"** At the time, in addition to working in the insurance industry, I was successfully running Gautreau's Restaurant and had recently produced an album for Island Records. I found myself explaining my various projects, and I was flattered by her interest in my career. Then she asked, "Why do you still sell insurance when you have all these other exciting things to do?" It was a compelling question, but in my mind, she had it all wrong. I was an insurance agent first and foremost; I loved the time I spent with clients helping to solve their problems. My real passion was relieving others of their burdens and helping them achieve clarity in their financial and personal pursuits. This is what I loved.

Name things you love about your job/career. Please make your answers as specific as possible. For example, regular tasks you enjoy performing.

_____

_____

_____

_____

(Circle the 3 things you like most from the above list.)

Name things you dislike about your job/career. Please make your answers as specific as possible. For example, regular tasks you hate performing.

_____

_____

_____

_____

(Circle the 3 things you dislike most from the above list.)

Passion is commonly associated with love. However, it originated from the Latin word *pati*, to suffer. Perhaps the lesson in the word's etymology is that the pursuit of passion will most likely create challenges. Therein lies the dilemma. In order to achieve your ultimate goals, there will be obstacles. Running away from these obstacles will only leave you to wonder what could have been. But, using your vision and your passion to overcome those challenges should lead to long-term success.

Shortly before I sold my insurance business to a bank, I went to breakfast with my cousin (of my father's generation) who is also in the insurance business. Trying to be helpful, he explained to me the potential financial rewards of using the bank to prospect for insurance clients. He encouraged me to continue selling insurance for the bank. Though grateful for the advice, I explained to him that my heart was just not in it. My passion was to help clients achieve their goals. So I sold my business and focused on freeing Gullivers. While this passion cost me money in the short run, after four years, it has enriched me beyond my highest expectations.

To begin to discover your passions and address the challenges that may await, answer the following questions.

If money were no concern, what opportunities would you pursue?

_____

_____

_____

What other constraints besides money keep you from pursuing each of these opportunities?

_____

_____

_____

How much money would you need to pursue each of these opportunities now?

_____

What if you were to allow your passion to drive you? Are you doing that now, or are you keeping it bottled up until the day you have "enough time"? Another word derived from the root *pati* is patience. Patience is a virtue; you'll need it to endure the challenges necessary for pursuing your passions. But patiently waiting for the perfect moment is no virtue at all. The longer you wait, the longer you avoid living your fullest life—and the more empty you feel.

Remember when you were first going out into the world on your own? Didn't you feel as if you were starting fresh and all possibilities were open to you? Weren't you convinced that no matter which path you chose, you'd surely achieve success? Unfortunately, that newfound freedom is usually quickly followed by confusion. With so many paths to choose from, which way should you go? You might panic and choose the wrong road. You might look up 30 years later and find yourself still plodding along, still not sure why. The clarity you'll gain by identifying your passion will act as your fuel, powering you down the path that is right for you.

BEN & MICHELLE

Ben and Michelle were clearly in need of more fuel by the time I came along. They had been married for 15 years and had three wonderful children. Ben had run a successful construction company that he had grown into one of the largest in the state. Michelle had graduated with an MBA in finance and had gone to work for a large bank. When their first child came, she quit working outside the home. Now that their third child was in school, Michelle was looking to get back into the business environment. In 1999, they began to rethink their life goals. Ben thought that he would be happier with less stress in his life and more time with the family. He knew he could sell his business, and given the market conditions at the time, could retire and still provide for his family. In addition, he would have time to build that dream home he and Michelle had always wanted, on some country property they owned. They both envisioned a beautiful place where their kids could run around with no worries. They had already stocked the small pond and were looking forward to some good fishing in the years to come.

So in 2000, Ben sold his business to focus on this new vision. The only problem was that shortly thereafter the market crashed and Ben and Michelle's plans were shattered. By the time I met them two years later, they had lost all passion for their new vision. Ben was still working for the company he had sold. Ben's wealth before the crash had allowed them to live comfortably without any real planning, but now they were left feeling uncertain and vulnerable. Their money had so dwindled that they felt hopeless, overwhelmed, so tied down by unknowns that they were not sure where to begin. Ben and Michelle had run out of gas.

The first thing we did was focus on Ben's true passions. Ben had enjoyed building his business and loved the detailed work involved in growing a large business. He decided that retirement (which we will discuss in more detail in Lesson 6) was not what he really wanted, even though it had been the driving force behind his original plan. I worked with Ben and Michelle to help them clarify their vision. They both felt that they would like to start a business using their knowledge of the construction industry to help people. After many meetings, we decided that retirement and their dream house were projects that could wait. We stabilized Michelle and Ben's investments and began to bring some order back to their life. They are in the midst of writing a business plan and are ready to apply their passions to the new enterprise. They are refueled and ready for their new journey.

It took a crash landing for Ben and Michelle to discover the importance of clarity. You may never face such a crash, but you should have a parachute ready in case you do. Ben and Michelle will be the first to tell you that clear objectives make for a soft landing.

Throughout time, adventurers have sought to conquer new horizons. It's never possible to actually reach the horizon, of course, but that is not the point. It is the quest, not the end result, that matters.

Like those adventurers, you must always know why you're going, even though you may not know exactly where your life road will lead. These questions will help you figure this out.

List things you would like to do more often.

_____

_____

What is keeping you from doing each of these things more often?

_____

_____

When is the next time you plan to do each of these things?

_____

_____

_____

In his memoir, *Into Thin Air*, Jon Krakauer believes that those who trekked to the top of Mount Everest for recognition, rather than for passion, were responsible for the deaths of many climbers. Theirs was not a pursuit of passion, but a pursuit of ego. They wanted bragging rights. They wanted to be able to say they'd climbed the world's highest peak, but they didn't want to put in the hard work it takes to achieve those great results.

People who allow passions to energize them are more likely to succeed because they have these passions fueling their journey, and they're committed to reaching the summit. People who are driven by ego have less success because their energy fades quickly. Overnight successes are rare. The success we see in others is usually just the peak of the mountain. We often pay attention to the rewards; only rarely do we glimpse the sacrifices.

Are you climbing your own metaphorical Mount Everest because you love the challenge? Are you inspired by those who went before? Or are you most interested in telling people how rich, how tough, how adventurous you are? You'll regret it if you get to the top only to realize you climbed the wrong mountain.

STUART

Stuart was about to climb the wrong mountain. He had recently sold his business and had a lot of money to invest. His situation was well known in his community, so he was fielding a lot of requests for money to seed new businesses. When I met with Stuart, he was excited about some of these investment opportunities. I was puzzled by his enthusiasm, though, since none of these investments seemed to offer rewards commensurate with their risks. (We will discuss risk more in Lesson 5.) I couldn't imagine why Stuart was so excited about these prospects, especially his first choice of investments, part ownership in a fast-food chain. He had already told me that dislike of operations had contributed to his decision to sell his business. So I asked him, "Why would you want to get bogged down in the minutiae of running a fast-food chain, especially when you'll need at least a hundred stores just to make a return on your investment?"

Stuart replied that he thought it would be fun to be active in business again.

I looked at him for a moment, surprised. "So you want to be active in business?"

"Yes," he replied.

"Well," I reminded him, "you already are." Stuart was running his family investment fund, and he seemed to enjoy the diverse challenges of that business. He had been so busy looking at the other peaks—the ones on that unattainable horizon—that he forgot how much he enjoyed the trek he was already making.

THE LEAP IS NEVER AS BIG AS YOU THINK IT IS

The discovery of passion is an adventure, and in any true adventure you never know what's coming next. In the movies, the hero always succeeds. That's not real life. In fact, no one knows for certain where their life will take them. You may not make it off the mountain. You will always be tempted to stay with your old "normal." After all, it is the safe place to be. Change is hard and there will always be a reason to keep things as they are. Now might not be the time for a big change. But there will always be reasons for staying in your comfort zone instead of starting out for your "new normal" and having to live with some temporary discomfort. Remember, the leap is never as big as you think it is.

Let's see what some of your leaps have looked like.

List the greatest accomplishments of your life.

_____

_____

_____

_____

List the greatest disappointments of your life.

_____

_____

_____

_____

Having a clear vision and a passion for that vision makes all the difference. If you believe, as I do, that your passion is what drives you—your fuel—then ignoring it can cause serious repercussions. Have you ever been in a car that has run out of gas? It is not a good feeling. Like the car, those who deny their passion will always be a little empty. They may be tempted to blame others for their dilemma instead of looking within themselves. Think of Dorothy in *The Wizard of Oz*. She made a grueling journey down the yellow brick road, trying only to get home. Ultimately she learned that her passage home was inside herself all along, and that happiness awaited her, right in her own backyard.

What's in your backyard?

List the 5 things you are most passionate about from your previous answers.

_____

_____

_____

_____

Are you currently making the most of these passions in your life? Why or why not?

_____

_____

_____

Write one way you can utilize these passions more in the next week.

_____

_____

Write one way you can utilize these passions more in the next year.

_____

_____

LESSON

4

LEGACY

*The legacy of heroes is the memory of a great name
and the inheritance of a great example.*
—Benjamin Disraeli

Now that you've identified your vision of success, your passion and your location, it's time to consider the end of your journey. Chances are, in your mind, your end game has more to do with retirement from work and less to do with your ultimate retirement: death. What a frightening word. Its mere vocalization makes us shiver. However, try as we might, no matter how much Botox we inject, death is inevitable. What will people say about the life you've led? How will you be remembered? If only you had spent as much time planning your legacy as you did planning your finances. Remember, it is important to live your legacy, not just to leave one. Don't fret. It's never too late (or too soon) to start.

LEGACY: LIVE IT OR LEAVE IT?

Let's first discuss family legacy. I see estate planning as playing a part in, but not embodying, the concept of family legacy. Think about a deceased relative who made a big impression on you; I'm sure one or two will spring immediately to mind. Whether you realize it or not, they left you their legacies, which you've probably been carrying out for them in the way you live your life.

When I think of family legacy, I think back to my grandfather, who kept a family Bible outlining our family tree. It was filled with the births, marriages and deaths of everyone in our family, going back generations. I remember reading through the names with my grandfather and discussing my ancestors. My family was from Natchez, Mississippi, and I learned mostly about my great-great grandfather, Henry Frank, for whom my son is named. He was an interesting man who sent all of his sons to Phillips Exeter Academy in New Hampshire and then on to Yale. In fact, when I went to Exeter I was the fourth generation to do so. Then there was my great-great uncle, Harry Frank. He was the black sheep of the family who ran away to Mexico to avoid a world of problems and was never heard from again. One of the greatest gifts my grandfather left me when he died was that family Bible, and I look forward to sharing it with my grandchildren in the future.

I've tried to start some new family traditions with my children. I try to plan special trips and outings with each of them individually—just the two of us. My 11-year-old son Henry and I plan to travel to one away game each year to see our home team, the New Orleans Hornets, play basketball. Each year we'll visit a different arena in a different city. There are 30 teams in the league, so if we stick to our plan, for the next 29 years we'll be alone together for at least one weekend a year. Who knows? I might be taking along some grandchildren to some of those games.

Once a month, Henry and his older sister Patti get to sleep in because their school does not start until 9 a.m., while Kate, who is in fifth grade, has to be there at 8 a.m. So one Wednesday a month, Kate and I go to breakfast at our favorite spot, just the two of us. We talk about important fifth-grade things, like who is mad at whom and what are the latest trends in girl hairstyles.

When my children were younger, each one had a full Saturday a couple of times a year to do with me whatever he or she wanted. We would go to the mall, to a movie, the zoo, hang out in the park throwing the football, or just have lunch together. I'll let you in on a secret: I had as much fun as they did. It was a great way to spend time with my kids individually and really interact with them in a significant way.

Patti is now 14; those of you with teenagers know spending time with dad is not always cool. This year, she is helping the high school football team as one of the assistant trainers. What this really means is that she brings water out to the team at timeouts. I am usually at every game and after the game come over to see what her plans are for the night. Like all dads, I want my hug. I have been informed that there will be no public displays of affection until the football players leave the field. She will give me that hug when no one is watching, though. They do grow up, but the time you spend with them pays dividends bigger than that you will ever receive from any investment you will ever make.

What traditions are you starting for your family? How much time are you spending with your kids, your nieces and nephews, and how involved are you in their development? Your ultimate legacy is your family; they are your living and growing tribute. Make sure you devote yourself to your family legacy; it's the best investment you can make. These questions will help you begin the process.

List some of the most important life lessons you wish to pass on to your children.

_____

_____

_____

_____

Do you think they already understand these?

_____

If not, how do you plan to impart these lessons?

_____

_____

_____

List the most important things you want your children to remember about you.

_____

_____

_____

_____

Do they already know these things?

_____

If not, when do you plan to tell them?

_____

Many people, especially in today's world, view estate planning and legacy planning as the same thing. To most, it's about managing their money to leave for their heirs. Yet these same people worry about the negative effects an inheritance might have. **The attitude you take toward money affects your family and your family legacy.**

What principles of money management would you want your children to follow? Rank in order those that are important to you with 1 being the most important.

_____ **Have fun; don't be afraid to spend it**

_____ **Be willing to take risks**

_____ **Help others**

_____ **Save for a rainy day**

_____ **Live within your means**

_____ **Live debt free**

_____ **Other** _____

I had a client, Richard, who was worried that money would spoil his children. He was a successful businessman who had grown a small family business into a large multinational company, which he ultimately sold. As we discussed his concerns, he came to realize that money itself doesn't spoil children—but negative behaviors and attitudes about money often do. For example, what message is conveyed when mom and dad are always away on business, choosing to spend a few extra days away from home to finalize a deal rather than getting home in time for their daughter's soccer game? The deal may be important, but is it more important than the child? You may tell yourself that you're missing only one game, but the child believes that business (and, by extension, money) is more important than she is. Kate still remembers that I cut short an important meeting in order to watch her championship baseball game (which she won, by the way). It was a treat for both of us, an experience we still recount today.

My client, Richard, remained committed to his business, but he made it a policy to take off every time his kids had a vacation day during the school year to spend time with them. He showed them by his actions that they were more important than his business, and, in turn, they matured into terrific, productive young people.

I know of another man, who runs a subsidiary of a large public company, who also sets work aside in order to spend time with his family. It's well known among his employees that he leaves the office every day at 6:30 to get home in time for dinner. His employees know that if they need something from him, they'd better have it to him before 6:30. It is an absolute rule he lives by, and everyone he works with adjusts accordingly. It is a point of pride for him. He believes that his business life can adjust to his family life—not the other way around—and he is right.

You may not be able to leave work for every school holiday, or attend every event in which your child participates. But you must find a way to spend time with your family and be an active participant in their lives, not just a casual observer. Don't underestimate the value of the efforts you make to balance your family time with your work. Such gestures, however small they may seem at the time, leave a lasting impression and serve as a positive illustration of your priorities.

By emphasizing the personal aspects of family legacy, I do not mean to trivialize the financial nuts and bolts of estate planning. The process of dividing assets and writing a sound will are vital aspects of your legacy. But always keep the former in mind when considering the latter, which we will do now.

A lot of people don't realize that we all have wills, whether we've written one or not. If you die without leaving a will (intestate), don't worry—the state has one for you. Unfortunately, it might not divide your property as you want it divided.

EILEEN

Eileen came to me after the death of her husband, Jonathan, who had not left a will for the few assets they owned. Jonathan had a son from his first marriage, and Eileen and Jonathan had a daughter together. Under Louisiana law, half the assets were Eileen's and the other half went into her husband's estate. Because there was no will, his estate was split between his two children, but Eileen had the right to use the assets for the rest of her life. The arrangement seemed reasonable until Eileen decided to sell her house. Since all she owned outright was 50 percent of the property, she had to get her stepson's permission to sell. Even though he had no right to the assets until her death, as a partial owner of the house he had to agree to the sale. Eileen and her stepson had a bit of a strained relationship, which meant that for Eileen to sell the house she needed to give up 25 percent of her equity in her home to her stepson so he would sign the papers. Had Jonathan and Eileen planned ahead, the property could have been left in a trust, and this problem could have been avoided.

To which of the following would you prefer your estate be distributed after your death? Rank in order of importance with 1 being the most important.

_____ Spouse	_____ Charitable Organization
_____ Children	_____ Religious Institution
_____ Parents	_____ Family Foundation
_____ Other Relatives	_____ Civic Organization
_____ Grandchildren	_____ Other

Eileen's was a simple problem; we've all heard worse stories, some that even sound like nightmares. A well-planned will allows you and your family to sleep soundly. As a simple, legal declaration of how your assets are to be divided, a will lessens the possibility of posthumous arguments over your assets. However, sometimes this seemingly simple exercise is not so simple. One of the first issues I bring up with my clients is the issue of fair versus equal division of assets. It is important to realize that these two concepts are not the same.

I had a client, Robert, with three children, only one of whom worked in their small family business. Let's say the business was worth $500,000, and Robert's total estate was worth $1.5 million. He and his wife wanted everything to be divided equally, so their will divided the estate into equal thirds—an equal division, but not fair. With all assets divided into thirds, the child who worked in the family business would be only a minority shareholder (with 33 percent ownership). It would have been more fair to leave him the business outright and let the other children split the remaining assets (each child, then, would inherit assets valued at $500,000).

In estate planning, fair is not always equal and equal is not always fair. What do you believe about this?

☐ **Regardless of my heirs' individual circumstances or needs, each child should receive an equal share of my estate.**

☐ **Based on the individual needs and circumstances of each of my heirs, an appropriate share should be distributed from my estate.**

BURDEN OR BENEFIT?

Don't forget to consider what financial principles you want your heirs to follow. Are they equipped to handle the money they inherit? If you don't know your family, if you haven't been an active participant in their lives, you may not be able to answer this question. Let's say you have two children with very distinct personalities. One is responsible and independent, while the other is confused and struggling. The second child has absolutely no ability to handle wealth, yet you want very much to treat both children fairly and equally. The simple solution is to leave the troubled child's money in a trust managed by a bank. The child will get all the income from the principal, and the trustee has the ability to spend from the principal for health, education, or other general welfare needs. Whether $50,000 or $50 million, money left outright to children who can't handle it is a burden, not a gift.

How do you feel about your heirs' ability to manage money?

☐ **My heirs are too young to manage money right now.**

☐ **My heirs are old enough to manage money, but they are not responsible with it.**

☐ **My heirs are old enough to manage money, and they can do it responsibly.**

Most of us want to leave our heirs with the opportunity and motivation to succeed on their own. Those of you who have built your own wealth know the pride that comes with such an accomplishment. Remember that pride as you plan your will. The last thing you want to do is leave an inheritance that diminishes your heirs' initiative to be productive. As Warren Buffet stated, "You want your children to have enough money so they can do anything, but not so much that they can do nothing."

What do you believe about leaving money to your children, and how it may affect them? (Check all items you agree with.)

☐ If children are given too large of an inheritance, they are likely to lead less productive lives and may even suffer a loss of self-worth, as well as a lack of respect from others.

☐ My children would take what I give them and be responsible with it.

☐ I would be concerned about leaving a large inheritance to my heirs because it could be squandered through poor management, divorce, or poor financial advice.

☐ Children should earn their own way. As the person who has accumulated my money, I would like to direct it toward charitable organizations now and after my death.

☐ I believe my children presently feel "entitled" to my estate, but I am confident they will get over any disappointment if their inheritance fails to meet their expectations.

☐ Children develop more positive values if they are not left a significant amount of wealth.

☐ Unlike my own parents, who were unable or unwilling to leave me a significant inheritance, if possible, I would like to give my children the advantage money provides.

☐ Regardless of their individual needs, parents should leave children the maximum possible inheritance.

☐ If possible, parents should leave children the minimum inheritance required to meet their individual lifestyle needs.

☐ Parents should not leave their children an inheritance.

In addition to a standard will, you should consider leaving what I call an **ethical will**. Although not legally enforceable, an ethical will is a valuable document. It tells your heirs what is important to you and why. A very personal document, your ethical will can be as short as a paragraph or as long as 10 pages. It can talk about issues as mundane as your personal articles or as lofty as your aspirations for your heirs. Most of all, I believe your ethical will serves as a platform to share your values and wishes with those you leave behind.

VICTORIA

Victoria is a client who has three children and a fairly large estate. She has given many monetary gifts to her children and grandchildren over the years. I asked her two questions that I ask all my clients: "If you were to list the most important things you want your children to remember about you, would they already know most of them? If not, when do you plan on telling them?" After some discussion, Victoria decided that what she wanted most was to be remembered as a parent who had tried her best. She decided to write each child a letter detailing the things she most appreciated about them. She intends to leave these letters in her will. To further the point of living a legacy versus leaving one, I have urged her to send the letters while she is still alive.

CHARITY BEGINS AT HOME

Another vital part of estate planning is your social, or community, legacy. I hope that you have some affiliation with a school, church, or civic organization that is important to you. If so, congratulations. If not, start one now. As federal budgets get tighter and states begin to feel the pinch, it becomes increasingly important for citizens to support causes they deem valuable. Whether you choose to contribute monetarily or by volunteering your time and talents, you will leave your mark by giving back to your community. Volunteering helps to build strong, cohesive societies. The more you invest in your community, the more you can expect from it. If you live a life marked by social activism, you will surely leave a legacy of generosity and altruism.

What do you think about donating to charitable organizations during your lifetime, when you can see the immediate impacts of your gifts?

☐ I would like to make gifts as soon as possible.

☐ I would like to make some gifts today, but would also like to explore tools such as charitable trusts to achieve philanthropic as well as other financial objectives.

☐ I would like to make some gifts today, but will donate a larger portion of my assets at my death.

☐ I do not plan to make charitable contributions.

What organizations would you give to? List some of the most important.

_____

_____

_____

_____

GIVING BACK

When I was growing up, my mother used to adopt a needy family for Christmas every year. She did not simply donate money but took us shopping for the adopted family's presents. The impact of my mother's lessons on my life has been invaluable, enforcing the idea of donating both time and money to a worthy cause. It helped inspire me to become one of the founders of the Young Leadership Council, which now has more than 1,000 members and has raised millions for charitable organizations in New Orleans. I have strived to continue the family tradition with Patti, Henry and Kate by constantly preaching to them the need to give back to your community.

And while it might not appear your children are always listening, sometimes they will surprise you. One day, a young boy knocked on our door. My wife answered it; Henry, 10 at the time, was right behind her. It seemed the young boy was going door-to-door collecting money so he could go back to summer camp. He showed Heidi and Henry pictures of him taken at camp the previous summer. Unfortunately, my wife only had $2 on her at the time, but she gave that to him. When Henry asked her how much she had given the boy, Heidi told him. Henry had been to camp for the first time that past summer and had loved it. So he went upstairs and got $20, which was all of his money, ran outside, caught up with the little boy and gave it to him.

Heidi only found out about it when she asked him where he had gone. I guess he had been listening.

What do you think about volunteerism and other forms of philanthropy as a family objective?
Check all that apply.

☐ Charitable giving (of time and money) is an individual thing and does not work well as a shared experience.

☐ Achieving a family consensus around giving is essential to successful family philanthropy.

☐ Irrespective of consensus, all members of the family should be provided with resources to give to charitable organizations as they see fit.

☐ A family foundation will enhance the process of family philanthropy by creating an entity in which all family members can play an important decision-making role.

☐ A family foundation is unnecessarily complicated and not required for effective family philanthropy.

☐ Shared philanthropy provides an opportunity to use actions, not just words, to teach children what is important.

Is charitable giving and/or volunteerism a value you wish to pass on to your children?

I advise all my clients to leave some portion of their assets in a family foundation. If you have a substantial sum of money, you can establish your own foundation. If not, most communities have organizations, known as supporting foundations, that will create a foundation for your family under their umbrella. Money left to a foundation is not taxed in your estate, which essentially means that the government, by giving up its revenue, is adding to your contribution. I can't imagine a better way for your heirs to continue your charitable principles than by gathering yearly to select the charities that will benefit from your gift.

KEVIN

As you think about what kind of legacy you want to leave, I'd like you to consider the story of Kevin, a prominent and affluent member of the community. After he passed away, everyone in his church congregation was gossiping about how much money he had left in his will; in fact, it was the talk of the town. One Sunday, while delivering his sermon, the minister mentioned the recently deceased member. He told the congregation that he knew exactly how much the man had left. There was rapt silence as those present waited to hear the sum. "All of it," said the minister. "He left all of it behind." We must remember that the old saying is true: "You can't take it with you." Only the example of our actions and the values we have instilled in others will remain. There is no better time than now to begin to live your legacy. If you live life to the fullest, establish clarity of vision and follow your passions, your legacy will surely be great.

What will your legacy be?

_____

_____

_____

RISK

Risk is a word that can mean different things to different people. In the basic tenets of financial planning, risk is defined as the financial uncertainty that the actual return on an investment will be different from the expected return. In other words, in order to make money you have to take the chance of losing it. I take a different approach. I think of risk as more than an equation of how much chance you're willing to take in order to a get a certain reward. I believe **there can also be a risk in not taking action.**

List some of the biggest personal risks you have taken.

_____

_____

_____

_____

What did you learn from taking these risks?

_____

_____

_____

List the biggest financial risks you have taken.

_____

_____

_____

_____

What did you learn from taking these risks?

_____

_____

_____

W H A T   A R E   Y O U   W I L L I N G
T O   L O S E ?

I attended an insurance meeting many years back where a hospice worker spoke. The most interesting thing she shared was the number-one regret of most of her dying patients. It wasn't "I wish I had spent more time with my family," or "I wish I had traveled more and seen more places." The most common regret was "I wish I had taken more risks."

With this in mind, let's explore risk and how it can be viewed in the context of a thorough financial plan. I tell my clients that more important than what they are willing to risk is what they are willing to lose. During the heyday of the stock market in the late 1990s, everyone seemed willing to take risks. I am convinced that this was due to the popular (and incorrect) belief that the market couldn't possibly go down. Ask those investors now about their tolerance for risk; the answer is probably quite different than it was in the late '90s.

To illustrate this point, I often ask my clients (and you should ask yourself), "If you could take all your money and have a 50 percent chance of doubling it, but also a 50 percent chance of losing it all, would you do it?" Everyone I've asked has answered no. Next I ask, "How much would you be willing to wager?" When they come up with an amount, my clients have begun to understand their appetite for risk.

More important than how much risk you're willing to take, however, is how much risk you need to take. The difference between these two amounts is critical to your financial plan. On a scale of one to ten, where are you in achieving your financial goals? If you've determined your location by answering the questions at the end of Lesson 2, you should know the answer. You should also have a clear vision of your goals. Now you can begin to determine how much risk you need to take to achieve those goals.

List some of your current personal and financial goals.

_____

_____

_____

_____

Where do you think you are in meeting your financial goals, with 1 being "I am doing a terrible job" and 10 being "I am doing the best job possible"?

1   2   3   4   5   6   7   8   9   10

This is the part of the planning process that can get technical. You need as much information as possible in order to make sound decisions; some form of statistical analysis is a necessary component of that information. I use Monte Carlo simulation software, an industry standard, to better understand risk as it relates to reward. This and similar programs are based on probabilities and use statistics to make predictions. Though they cannot tell you exactly how much money you will have at specific points in the future, they can tell you the probability of achieving certain results.

An example: if you invested $100,000 in the S&P 500 index from 1984 through 2003, you would have averaged 14.3 percent return each year. However, the return ranged from a high of 37.54 percent in 1995 to a low of –23.37 percent in 2002. This measurement of volatility is called standard deviation. For the S&P 500 index, the standard deviation was 17.10. The lower the standard deviation, the less volatility there is in the return. For instance, the standard deviation of treasuries, one of the least risky investments, for the last 20 years (as measured by the Lehman Midterm index) was only 5.22. The return for the treasuries was 8.46 percent, almost 6 percent below the S&P return, with the high being 18.16 percent in 1985 and the low being –2.56 percent in 1994.

Using the S&P 500 index return of 14.3 percent and its standard deviation of 17.1, the Monte Carlo analysis tells us that the $100,000 invested in the S&P 500 index will have 100 percent chance of being between $124,878.67 and $2,160,687.97 at the end of twenty years.

Obviously, this is a wide range. A better picture is that we have an 80 percent chance of being between $321,672 and $1,447,733. Conversely, if we were to invest in treasuries instead of equities, we would have a 100 percent chance of being between $233,866.24 and $560,480.60. As you can see, the less risky investment ensures less loss, but likewise limits your possible gain. Using analysis such as Monte Carlo simulation allows you to construct your portfolio based on your personal appetite for risk.

Once your necessary level of risk has been determined, you can decide how much risk you are willing to take. Now things really start to get interesting. Assess your willingness to take a risk on the one-to-ten scale, with one being dipping a single toe in the water, and ten being gung-ho, ready to dive in head first. Often my clients are willing to take the risks necessary to achieve their goals, and we can move on to the planning stage. But just as often they're not, and I have to coax them into the water a little bit at a time.

GEORGE

George is a businessman with two grown children. He had never been a big earner but had done well enough over the years to accumulate a decent portfolio. After we discussed his needs and goals, George realized that he needed to take more risk than he was willing to take. Rather than go back and readjust his portfolio in order to try to achieve his desired results, George tried changing some of his financial assumptions. In the process of reviewing his financial situation, George realized that he could tighten his budget, save more, and ultimately achieve his goals without increasing his risk. Remember, you don't have to take more risk than you are comfortable taking; there are usually other ways to achieve the results you want.

Every so often clients believe that they are very close (eight or nine on a scale of one to ten) to meeting their financial goals. For the most part these clients have a large net worth. Naturally, they feel that they need to take very little risk. When I ask them how much risk they are willing to take, however, they often respond with, "a fair amount." **Why would anyone be willing to take more risk than they needed to take?** Other than the adrenaline freak who loves risk for risk's sake, most of us would never choose to take more risk than necessary. After years of talking with clients who fit this profile, an answer struck me: though most were embarrassed to say so, as rich as these clients were, they wanted to be richer. In truth, they were not really at eight or nine on their financial-goal scale—they were closer to five or six. Thus, they did need to take more risk, and their willingness and needs did match up—they just weren't being honest about what they wanted.

How much risk are you willing to take to meet your goals? Rate this risk below, with 1 being "I am not willing to take any risk" and 10 being "I am willing to risk everything."

1   2   3   4   5   6   7   8   9   10

How much risk do you think you need to take to meet your goals? Rate this risk below, with 1 being "I do not need to take any risk" and 10 being "I need to risk everything."

1   2   3   4   5   6   7   8   9   10

IS YOUR NEST EGG HARD-BOILED?

You must be honest with yourself about your goals, whether you have $20,000,000 or $20,000. If you don't plan for what you really want, you might take more risk than necessary, or you might not take enough. Remember not to use value judgments in assessing your goals. Those clients who seemed to have enough wanted more for various valid reasons. One wanted to be able to give more to charity; another wanted to keep growing his business. If you follow the *FreeGulliver* philosophy—clarify your vision, establish your location, identify your passion—you can move forward productively rather than work against your true desires.

The amount of risk you can and should take is also dependent on how much time you have to achieve your goals. Let's play with the old cliché that refers to one's savings as a "nest egg." Think of a raw egg as risky and a hard-boiled egg as safe. The longer you cook the egg, the harder, or safer, it will become. Thus an investment, which may be risky over a one-year term, gets safer if assessed over 20 years.

Take equities as an example. For any given year, a portfolio of stocks could lose as much as 20 percent. In fact, in 2002 the S&P was down 23.37 percent. However, over any 20-year history since the S&P has been tracked (1926), the index has never lost money. Never. As of 2002, the smallest 20-year return has been three percent. I can't guarantee that the next 20 years will be like the past. But if the past is any indication, time makes a risky investment a whole lot safer.

Finally, let me reintroduce you to a term you're probably already somewhat familiar with: **diversification**. You cannot make a sound financial plan without it.

Despite your assessment of how much risk you should take, risk may sometimes take you. There are several classes of investment risk, including one that has reared its ugly head the last few years: market risk. Market risk refers to the possibility that the value of your portfolio can go up or down. **Inflation risk** refers to the possibility that prices will rise, decreasing consumers' ability to purchase goods and services. **Interest-rate risk** relates to increases or decreases in prevailing interest rates, which result in price fluctuation of investments, particularly bonds. There is an inverse relationship between bond prices and interest rates, so as interest rates rise, bond prices fall, and vice-versa. The risk of loss in this case is not as much of a concern if you hold a bond to maturity; however, if you need to sell a bond prior to maturity and interest rates have risen, there is a risk that the bond will be worth less than you paid. **Credit risk** refers to the economic viability of your investment. For example, a bond issuer may not be able to service its payment or a publicly traded company may declare bankruptcy. All investments involve some level of credit risk.

Before you let this information depress you, let me remind you that there is a way to protect against all these risks: that old buzzword, diversification. Your investments must be diversified by asset class and by correlation (the relationship between two classes of assets). For example, a mid-cap investment (stocks in mid-sized companies) is highly correlated to a large-cap investment (stocks in large companies). Ninety percent of the return of mid-cap stocks is explained by the return of large-cap stocks. Dividing your investments between mid-cap and large-cap may seem like diversification, but in fact this strategy does not provide protection from overall loss.

With the help of Monte Carlo simulations or similar software, it's possible to build a portfolio that, over time, will reach your objectives within your risk boundaries. But again, you must know what your goals are and which ones are non-negotiable. Can you continue to freely spend and still maintain your desired level of risk, or do you need to grow your savings? Is retirement really five years away, or should you try a new job that always interested you? Which risk would you rather take: one you choose for yourself, or one the market chooses for you? The risks my clients end up talking about most are the ones they wish they'd taken but didn't: the decision not to try that dream job because it didn't pay enough, the decision not to introduce a new product line because it didn't fit an original business plan. If you cut the strings that bind you, then the risk—and the rewards—will be up to you.

FAILURE IS
LEARNING TO SUCCEED

In dealing with all of my clients over the years I have begun to realize why many of them have not taken certain risks. It is the same reason most of us like to stay on the familiar side of "normal." We do not like to fail. No one does. However, without failure, there can be no growth. In our office, we have long since given up the notion that we will never be wrong. The one thing we know for certain is that we will make mistakes. I believe the only true failure is one from which you do not learn.

In November 2003, I was ready to make one of the biggest pitches of my life. My business partner (at the time) and I were meeting with the entire decision-making staff of a major publishing company to discuss our book. This was our second meeting and a deal was imminent. We prepared for the meeting, and we felt we were ready. We made our pitch, and I thought I had done a great job. I was feeling great. However, upon leaving the meeting, my partner was furious with me. She thought I had blown the meeting and ruined our chances for a deal. Obviously, we had been in different meetings. I was certain I had done a great job. Well, as it turned out, she had been at the right meeting. The company declined to publish our book; the reason was ME. They did not like me. I was devastated. I had let everyone down. I had failed. I was a "loser."

I had to come to grips with a central question of life: "How long do you hold on to failure before you let it go?" If you always blame others and never accept responsibility, then you will never learn and improve. I could have said that they were wrong and accepted no responsibility—that they were all idiots and just could not see my genius.

On the other hand, if you hold on to failure too long, it can consume you. We all know people with low self-esteem who cannot shake the feeling of failure. So I searched for the answer of how long to hold on to my failure. With the help of others, I figured out how long: Hold on to the failure for as long as it takes for the wisdom to pop out. My wisdom was a re-connection of my concepts and my book. The book I had presented was not the one I needed to write. It was more my partner and less me. It was a very different book.

The meeting caused our partnership to dissolve. But instead of quitting, I re-energized. I recommitted to my passion and got back to work. I spent six months writing my book. The lesson I learned from the failure resulted in my success. You are reading the book! I took a risk, had a failure, learned from it, and turned it into a success.

So if you're still afraid to take that toe out of the water and dive in, do not be. The worst that can happen is that you will fail. From this failure you will grow. Remember, once I had identified my passion and clarified my vision, I was ready to resume my journey and take the risks necessary to go forward. There were times when I threw caution to the wind, choosing my own path over the route suggested by others, even when those alternate routes were sound. Because I was doing what I love, I was especially energetic and dedicated at work. In only one year, the business was on track, and by year three I had replaced all the income I needed to support my family—which leads me to my final point about risk. Whatever level of risk you decide to take, don't forget that there are other people who will take it with you.

HOW SMALL?

When I come home from work, Heidi, my wife, always asks me how my day went. Back when I was selling insurance, there were often days when I could report a big new prospect or a lucrative sale. But in the early days of the new company, there wasn't as much exciting news to report. One day, after giving her the same answer—nothing had changed, but I loved what I did—I expressed my concern that I was not making enough money. My daughter Patti's ears pricked up with concern. "Dad, are we going to lose our house?" Laughing, I said no. But she had piqued my interest. I asked her if she would rather live in our large house with me in a job that made me unhappy, or in a smaller house with me in a job I loved. She thought about it a while and finally responded, "How small?" Her answer, while cute, is pertinent to our discussion of risk. She needed to assess the level of her sacrifice before she could decide. Luckily, we were able to have both a happy daddy and a large home. But I have never forgotten that the risks I take—and the discomfort that sometimes comes with them—are shared with my family.

You will minimize your investment risks with diversification; you will minimize your life-planning risks with clarity. Take some time to answer the following questions. Some will look familiar from previous lessons, but it's valuable to rethink them now as you consider your plans in the context of risk.

In trying to achieve your goals, what are the biggest risks you are facing right now?

_____

_____

_____

_____

Name some pros and cons of taking these risks.

_____

_____

_____

_____

What is the risk of not doing these things?

_____

_____

_____

_____

RETIREMENT

According to older dictionaries, the definition of retire is "to put out of service, to withdraw." Anyone who has been lucky enough to retire his debt knows this and hopes it never returns. But when your old car gets retired, it doesn't move to the beach. It ends up in the salvage yard. Given this definition, most people would not like to be retired. So how is it that retirement came to be seen as such a good thing? Everyone you talk to wants to retire by the time they reach 60. This book takes a different view of retirement by starting with a very simple premise: no one wants to retire from work they love. In order to deal with the issue of retirement, it is useful to go back in time and look at its history.

The notion of retirement was born in the early twentieth century. Before then, people simply worked until they died. Work was seen as an inextricable part of life; people worked to eat, stay productive and feel connected with their communities. In many societies, age was respected and older workers were valued for their experience and wisdom; they were seen as a resource and held an important place in the workforce.

Retirement has evolved in many phases throughout America's history and has changed dramatically since it was introduced. The original idea of retirement was a product of American industrialization, which ushered in a complete redefinition of the concept of work. This redefinition, which was rooted in the change from rural to urban life and from self-sufficiency to societal dependency, transformed older workers from a benefit to a liability. This notion was amplified during the Great Depression, when the unemployment rate climbed to more than 25 percent. Under President Franklin Roosevelt, the government created the Social Security Administration, hoping to effectively remove problematic older workers from the workforce and employ younger, more agile hands. In the earliest days of the program, Social Security payments were small, and retirement comprised a short period at the end of life. But the idea of retirement had taken root in the American consciousness.

The meager lifestyle initially afforded by retirement changed substantially with the myriad of economic shifts that occurred after World War II. Over time, retirement began to gain both years and glamour, earning the name "the Golden Years," which conjures images of sandy beaches, golf games and cocktails by the pool. This dazzling image of retirement helped to decrease the age of American retirees; the average age of retirement has plummeted from 70 in 1930 to 62 today. Along with the decrease in age came an increase in Social Security benefits and extended pension plans. Retirement was no longer a short period before death during which the elderly were forced to live on a tight budget, but an extended vacation without the responsibilities and worries of the workaday world.

With such a glamorous picture of retirement, it is not surprising that even as our life expectancy increases, our age of retirement keeps decreasing. If we start working at 22, expect to retire at 60 and live to age 82, then our retirement comprises almost 27 percent of our entire lives. The implications of this statistic are serious, both personally and financially—as well as for the national budget deficit. Many Americans are finding that the Golden Years are not all they're cracked up to be. Twenty-two years is a long time for an alert person to be without work.

ALLERGIC TO ROSES?

Beverly Sills, who enjoyed a long and respected career as a star soprano, retired from singing to become chair of Lincoln Center. In her early seventies she retired from that position, only to reappear six months later as chair of the Metropolitan Opera. "So I smelled the roses and developed an allergy," she told the *New York Times*. Ms. Sills, like most of us, did not want to be put out of service. Many people in their eighties lead productive, active lives, whether they're working or not. My grandfather died at 95 and worked until he was 92. He didn't do it for the money; he did it for the love of the work.

The financial implications of retirement are even more important. The average American's lifespan has increased from 48 in 1930 to 72 today. We no longer worry about living long enough to enjoy our retirement.

Now we worry about living so long that we run out of money. We have put a lot of pressure on ourselves to have a large nest egg ready for retirement. Out of fear, too many of us stay in jobs we hate in order to save a little more. I'll say it again—**staying in a job you hate is crazy**. Retirement planning should be more about lifestyle and less about finances.

When do you plan to take this next step in your life?

☐ **In the next five years**

☐ **In 6-10 years**

☐ **In 11-20 years**

☐ **In more than 21 years**

☐ **Other**_____

DOING WHAT YOU WANT WHEN YOU WANT

The first question I ask clients who want to talk about retirement is simple: Why? I try to get them to rethink the concept of retirement by defining the word. Most definitions I get are a variation of a simple idea:

"Doing what you want, when you want." Under this definition, most people who love their jobs are already retired. Look at Michael Jordan. Here is a man who so loved what he did that he refused to retire—in fact, he added two more championships to his name. Many celebrities, athletes, actors and television journalists continue to work well beyond the "pinnacle" of their careers. George Burns was still performing at 100. The combined ages of Mike Wallace and Morley Safer, two stalwarts of the most popular news magazine program on television, add up to almost 160. Katherine Hepburn was performing—and Julia Child cooking—well into their ninth decades. While they might not have had the success of their youth, they were still productive. Their love of their profession was so strong that they refused to quit. Why should you quit?

Next I ask my clients what part of their work they most enjoy. What would they like to continue doing into retirement? Most of us have in our jobs a few tasks we love, and the luckiest of us have a whole day filled with enjoyable activities. I ask my clients to identify these pleasurable activities, and then try to make those tasks compose a majority of their time at work. I once heard a great line that sums up this philosophy: **"Frank Sinatra**

did not move pianos." The point is clear: focus on your passions and talents, and try not to get bogged down in the chores you hate. If you concentrate on what you love and pursue it fully, your Golden Years can begin today.

A N D R E W

Andrew was the third-generation president of his family's company. At 50, he began losing his passion for running the business he had spent his entire life building. He thought it might be time to move on, but felt his son, William, wasn't quite old enough or experienced enough to take control. Andrew didn't think it would be fair to hire someone as president only to remove him or her a few years later when William was old enough to take the reins, so he resigned himself to running the company for another five or six years.

This issue came up when I was talking with Andrew about his estate planning. Given Andrew's net worth, I questioned why he'd want to keep working at a job he didn't like. Why not enjoy some of his hobbies while he was still energetic and healthy? I asked Andrew if he thought there might be potential buyers for the company. "Absolutely," Andrew said immediately. He estimated that he could sell the business fairly quickly for more money than he could ever spend. "I'm kind of torn," he said, "because I had the opportunity to inherit the business, and I want my son to have that opportunity as well. If it means I have to make a sacrifice, I'm willing to do that."

"What does William think about this?" I asked.

"I don't know," replied Andrew.

"Well, before you make this big sacrifice, don't you think you should find out what he wants?"

As it turned out, William did have a passion for the family business, just as his great-grandfather, grandfather and father had. He was frustrated, however, with his father's obvious lack of passion and energy, which was starting to affect employee morale. At the same time, he respected his father's experience and his efforts at building the company, and he knew he wasn't qualified to tell his father what to do.

Andrew and William sat down with me to discuss the situation. After a few hours, they each realized that there were things they liked about their jobs and things they didn't like. Andrew loved operations; William did not. William loved working with people, both employees and clients; Andrew was burned out from dealing with personnel problems and client issues. Neither Andrew nor William wanted to sell; they just wanted work to be fun again. They reorganized their responsibilities and delegated tasks according to their individual passions and preferences. They were re-energized. Retirement could wait.

Name things you would like to do in an ideal free week.

_____

_____

_____

_____

When was the last time you did these?

_____

When is the next time you plan to do these?

_____

How would you define a successful retirement? It's harder to do than you might think. We all know plenty of stories about people who have retired only to find themselves bored and unhappy. How many stories of happy retirements can you recall? Make a list of these success stories, and think about how these retirees made it work.

List people you think retired successfully.

_____

_____

_____

What makes their retirement successful?

_____

_____

Can this apply to you?

_____

THE RETIREMENT
REVOLUTION

We are in the midst of a retirement revolution. We are disillusioned with the idea of retiring to a life of idleness. For many of us, the idea of an extended vacation isn't compelling—in fact, it's a bit stifling. A growing number of retirees are dissatisfied with life after work; they want to stay active and engaged and continue to learn and grow. Today's retiree is energetic, vigorous and productive, and not about to settle into a life of inactivity and pointless leisure.

There is a lawyer I know in New Orleans who had always wanted to go into the Peace Corps. At age 64, he left a very successful law practice, and the firm which he had helped build into one of the largest in the region, to spend two years in Romania. He realized that it was never too late to follow your passions and that there was still too much work to be done to retire. I expect that as Baby Boomers move toward their "retirement" years, many others will follow a similar path, making time to devote to passions and causes rooted in earlier decades.

You might be saying to yourself, "Easier said than done." You have bills to pay, kids to educate—you can't just give up your income to chase your dreams. I don't disagree. **However, retirement doesn't have to be an all-or-nothing proposition.** In fact, it shouldn't be. If you are doing what you enjoy, you can do it for the rest of your life. You can, therefore, push back the date of your retirement.

Let's say you're staying in a job you hate because you're making $100,000 a year. After taxes, you bring home about $70,000. Now let's say you find a job you love, but it pays only $75,000 a year. Forget the fact that if you love your job, your income will probably rise. I would argue that you would excel in work you love and ultimately be more profitable. However, let's assume your salary stays relatively constant for the duration of your career. In other words, your salary rises, but only at the rate of the cost of living. With your dream job, after taxes you bring home $55,000 a year.

JOB YOU HATE (age 45)	JOB YOU LOVE
Bring home $70,000	Bring home $55,000
Save $20,000	Save $5000
Retirement Fund at 65 at 7%, $870,000	Retirement fund at 75 at 7%, 475,000
Income at 65 using 5% is $66,000	Making $55,000 for life

WHEN CAN I RETIRE?

The choice is clear: you can stay with a job you hate so you can save up enough to eventually quit, or you can start doing what you love now and just keep doing it. My bet is you will be having too much fun to retire.

Another question my clients frequently ask is "When

can I retire?" Using my definition of retirement, the answer may be "Sooner than you think." After the market crash of 2001, many of my clients were depressed that their savings had dropped to the point of almost vanishing.

Let's say you're 60 years old and have an income of $60,000 a year. The $600,000 you'd saved has evaporated to $300,000. Social Security will pay you $20,000 a year beginning at age 62. In order to retire with a comfortable income, you need $50,000 a year indexed for inflation. Thus, you need another $30,000 annually. With $600,000 in the bank you were fine, but with $300,000, you're about $15,000 a year short; you can take only five percent of your principal as income and still have some inflation protection.

Don't worry, you just need to change your thinking. For instance, there's at least one aspect of your work that you love, but if you adjust your job to do only that one function, your income will drop to $25,000 a year. Yes, it's a dramatic pay cut, but it's still more than you need to supplement your income from savings. You've eliminated the unpleasant aspects of your work, and you've achieved a comfortable income. And because you're doing only the work you love, you will work longer. As long as you're working, you'll continue to receive benefits. And with fewer years of actual retirement, you'll need less in principal savings from which to draw when you're no longer working. Get rid of the notion that work is bad and rest is good. To begin to rethink retirement, take some time to answer the questions below.

List the things you love most about what you do.

_____

_____

_____

_____

Do you love these things enough to continue doing them during your retirement?

_____

What percentages of your time do you spend on these activities?

_____

Considering all the things you like enough to do while in retirement, what do you think you could get paid to do just these tasks?

_____

List ways you think your lifestyle will change if you retire.

_____

_____

_____

_____

Are these good or bad changes?

_____

List things that you can do to start implementing good change now.

_____

_____

_____

_____

List ways you can either avoid bad changes completely or make them into something you see as good.

_____

_____

_____

_____

CONCLUSION

Making the simple complicated is commonplace; making the complicated simple, awesomely simple, that's creativity.
—Charles Mingus

Todd and Aimee came to me with a complicated dilemma. Though they had come to discuss their finances, we quickly realized that money was the least of their problems. Todd was a successful dealmaker who loved his work. Aimee was a CPA in a large local firm. They both were very good at what they did, but they felt they had reached an age where they wanted to slow down. They had three houses throughout the country but little time to enjoy them, their list of desired travel destinations was long, and they shared a lifelong dream to own a yacht. Their confusion as to how to achieve all their goals is typical of the Gullivers who walk through my door.

My first objective was to help Todd and Aimee gain clarity about their vision. What was truly important to them? It wasn't easy to sort out their various interests and business commitments. Financial planners may want everything to be nice and tidy, but life seldom is. Todd and Aimee wanted their investment strategy to center on their desire to travel. They knew that in order to travel more they would have to work less, but they worried about reducing their earnings too much. They thought, therefore, that their investments needed to be concentrated in income-producing assets to compensate for the income they would lose when they cut back their work hours.

They both emphasized a desire to be productive, and Todd told me there were still many business deals he was interested in pursuing. However, he felt that his passion for business was not what it once was. It was time for each of them to compose a passion statement. Both could identify aspects of their work they still loved, but they could name at least as many that they no longer enjoyed. This discovery led to a simple plan of action: Aimee quit her work at her firm and began to help Todd in his business. At the same time, they brought in a junior partner who was eager to do the tasks they both disliked. Everyone benefited, because the junior partner was passionate about all aspects of his work, and his energy improved operations and enhanced productivity. With this new solution in place, Todd and Aimee were able to take on even bigger projects and still have more time for travel.

With their vision and passions clarified, we were

able to move on to financial concerns. Todd and Aimee had been at a loss as to how to allocate their money in order to provide an ample income once they'd reduced their workload, but now they could see that semi-retirement would not necessarily zap their earning potential. With this clarity, we designed an allocation with slightly more aggressive investments to fit their new lifestyle.

It seemed as though everything had been resolved. Todd and Aimee's new life was running smoothly—until the yacht sailed back into the scene. With their other concerns addressed, they were ready to pursue this last aspect of their vision. However, they remained concerned about their ability to afford the day-to-day upkeep of a boat. I suggested the option of renting, but they felt strongly about owning one. They were willing to consider partnering with a friend, but the perfect boat became available before we were able to find the perfect partner. A decision needed to be made—and quickly.

As we worked on a plan to buy and finance the yacht, we had to consider Todd and Aimee's estate plan. Because they had no children, they had always planned to leave most of their estate to charity. With this goal in mind, we began to explore the potential problems yacht ownership might pose for this plan. In other words, would buying the boat so reduce their net worth that creating a meaningful foundation would be out of the question?

We determined that the yacht would consume less than 2.5 percent of their net worth over a two-year period. We then set a goal of two years for Todd and Aimee to find a partner so the boat's expenses would be more manageable. Finally, they would sell one of their houses to pay the deposit on the yacht and finance the balance. Once they had a sound financial plan in place, they could pursue their dream without fear. And though buying a yacht didn't maximize their wealth, I've never seen Todd and Aimee happier. They had clarified their vision, identified their passions, reassessed their financial situation, and determined how much risk they were willing to take in order to live their dream.

For Todd and Aimee it was a yacht. For you, it will be a different dream. However, Todd and Aimee's story illustrates an important point: in financial planning, everything is connected. You can't plan your investments without talking about retirement. You can't talk about retirement without considering risk; when determining how much risk you need to take, you have to consider the legacy you want to leave. And before you can tackle any of these concerns, you must have clarity: you must identify your vision, your passion, and your current location. Clarity leads to options, and options give you power. With clarity you are the captain of your own ship—just look at Todd and Aimee, who have literally steered a vessel toward a happier life.

As you reach the end of this book, I hope you are at the start of a new life: a life of clarity and vision, of passions fulfilled, and of financial freedom and responsibility. You'll understand how to define and align your personal, strategic and financial goals. Now it's time to start snipping away at all those pesky little strings that are tying you down. It's time to look at making that short leap to a "new normal." It's time to free your Gulliver.

If you have stories about how clarity has helped you simplify your own life or if you want to learn more about the Free Gulliver Process, please email us at trippfriedler@freegulliver.com or visit our website: www.freegulliver.com. We would love to hear from you.